The
Wiersbe
BIBLE STUDY SERIES

ACTS

The Wiersbe
BIBLE STUDY SERIES

Put Your

Faith

Where the

Action Is

David C Cook®
transforming lives together

THE WIERSBE BIBLE STUDY SERIES: ACTS
Published by David C Cook
4050 Lee Vance View
Colorado Springs, CO 80918 U.S.A.

David C Cook U.K., Kingsway Communications
Eastbourne, East Sussex BN23 6NT, England

The graphic circle C logo is a registered trademark of David C Cook.

All Scripture quotations in this study are taken from the *Holy Bible, New International Version of the Bible®. NIV®*. Copyright © 1973, 1978, 1984 by International Bible Society. Used by permission of Zondervan. All rights reserved.

In the *Be Dynamic* and *Be Daring* excerpts, unless otherwise noted, all Scripture quotations are taken from the King James Version of the Bible. (Public Domain.) Scripture quotations marked NASB are taken from the *New American Standard Bible*, © Copyright 1960, 1995 by The Lockman Foundation. Used by permission; and NKJV are taken from the New King James Version. Copyright © 1982 by Thomas Nelson, Inc. Used by permission. All rights reserved.

All excerpts taken from *Be Dynamic*, second edition, published by David C Cook in 2009 © 1987 Warren W. Wiersbe, ISBN 978-1-4347-6746-2; and *Be Daring*, second edition, published by David C. Cook in 2009 © 1988 Warren W. Wiersbe, ISBN 978-1-4347-6742-4.

ISBN 978-0-7814-0422-8
eISBN 978-0-7814-0559-1

© 2010 Warren W. Wiersbe

The Team: Steve Parolini, Karen Lee-Thorp, Amy Kiechlin, Jack Campbell, Karen Athen
Series Cover Design: John Hamilton Design
Cover Photo: iStockphoto

Printed in the United States of America
First Edition 2010

6 7 8 9 10 11 12 13 14 15

041316

Contents

Introduction to Acts

Be Dynamic

We call Dr. Luke's second volume "The Acts of the Apostles," when really it is the "Acts of God's People Empowered by the Holy Spirit." It is a story of power. God's people today share the same spiritual dynamic that energized the early saints. If we are yielded to the Spirit, we can be adding new chapters to the exciting story of the church.

There are some nonrepeatable events in Acts, as well as some transitional happenings; but the basic spiritual principles are the same today as when Peter and Paul ministered.

Be Daring

The eminent American psychologist William James said, "It is only by risking our persons from one hour to another that we live at all." And the popular motivational expert Earl Nightingale claimed, "Wherever there is danger, there lurks opportunity; wherever there is opportunity, there lurks danger."

Paul and his friends would say a hearty "Amen!" to these two statements and would back up their votes with the testimony of their lives.

After all, in the early church, Paul and Barnabas were known as "men who have risked their lives for the name of our Lord Jesus Christ" (Acts 15:26).

If we have the dynamic of the Holy Spirit in our lives, then surely we will not be satisfied with "Christian living as usual." We will want the Lord to put us where the real action is and make us daring pioneers instead of comfortable spectators.

We need to look to the essentials and discover afresh the spiritual dynamics of the Word of God and prayer, love and fellowship, persecution, and personal witness for Christ.

—*Warren W. Wiersbe*

How to Use This Study

This study is designed for both individual and small-group use. We've divided it into eight lessons—each references one or more chapters in Warren W. Wiersbe's commentaries *Be Dynamic* and *Be Daring* (second editions, David C. Cook, 2009). While reading *Be Dynamic* and *Be Daring* is not a prerequisite for going through this study, the additional insights and background Wiersbe offers can greatly enhance your study experience.

The **Getting Started** questions at the beginning of each lesson offer you an opportunity to record your first thoughts and reactions to the study text. This is an important step in the study process as those "first impressions" often include clues about what it is your heart is longing to discover.

The bulk of the study is found in the **Going Deeper** questions. These dive into the Bible text and, along with helpful excerpts from Wiersbe's commentary, help you examine not only the original context and meaning of the verses but also modern application.

Looking Inward narrows the focus down to your personal story. These intimate questions can be a bit uncomfortable at times, but don't shy away from honesty here. This is where you are asked to stand before the mirror of God's Word and look closely at what you see. It's the place to take a good look at yourself in light of the lesson and search for ways in which you can grow in faith.

Going Forward is the place where you can commit to paper those things you want or need to do in order to better live out the discoveries you made in the Looking Inward section. Don't skip or skim through this. Take the time to really consider what practical steps you might take to move closer to Christ. Then share your thoughts with a trusted friend who can act as an encourager and accountability partner.

Finally, there is a brief **Seeking Help** section to close the lesson. This is a reminder for you to invite God into your spiritual-growth process. If you choose to write out a prayer in this section, come back to it as you work through the lesson and continue to seek the Holy Spirit's guidance as you discover God's will for your life.

Tips for Small Groups

A small group is a dynamic thing. One week it might seem like a group of close-knit friends. The next it might seem more like a group of uncomfortable strangers. A small-group leader's role is to read these subtle changes and adjust the tone of the discussion accordingly.

Small groups need to be safe places for people to talk openly. It is through shared wrestling with difficult life issues that some of the greatest personal growth is discovered. But in order for the group to feel safe, participants need to know it's okay *not* to share sometimes. Always invite honest disclosure, but never force someone to speak if he or she isn't comfortable doing so. (A savvy leader will follow up later with a group member who isn't comfortable sharing in a group setting to see if a one-on-one discussion is more appropriate.)

Have volunteers take turns reading excerpts from Scripture or from the commentary. The more each person is involved even in the mundane tasks, the more they'll feel comfortable opening up in more meaningful ways.

The leader should watch the clock and keep the discussion moving. Sometimes there may be more Going Deeper questions than your group can cover in your available time. If you've had a fruitful discussion, it's okay to move on without finishing everything. And if you think the group is getting bogged down on a question or has taken off on a tangent, you can simply say, "Let's go on to question 5." Be sure to save at least ten to fifteen minutes for the Going Forward questions.

Finally, soak your group meetings in prayer—before you begin, during as needed, and always at the end of your time together.

Pentecost
(ACTS 1—2)

Before you begin ...
- *Pray for the Holy Spirit to reveal truth and wisdom as you go through this lesson.*
- *Read Acts 1—2. This lesson references chapters 1–2 in* Be Dynamic. *It will be helpful for you to have your Bible and a copy of the commentary available as you work through this lesson.*

Getting Started

From the Commentary

After His resurrection, Jesus remained on earth for forty days and ministered to His disciples. He had already opened their minds to understand the Old Testament message about Himself (Luke 24:44–48), but there were other lessons they needed to learn before they could launch out in their new ministry. Jesus appeared and disappeared during those forty days, and the believers never knew when He might show up. It was excellent preparation for the church because the days were soon coming when He would no longer be on earth to instruct them personally. We believers today never know when our Lord may return, so our situation is somewhat similar to theirs.

—*Be Dynamic,* page 20

1. Read Acts 1:1–11. How is Jesus' postresurrection teaching represented in the book of Acts? Why do you think it was so important for the church that Jesus continued to minister after His resurrection? How is our situation similar to that of the early church?

More to Consider: Read Romans 10:9–10 and 1 Corinthians 15:1–8, 16–19. What do these verses tell us about the importance of Jesus' resurrection? How might the early church have suffered if people didn't believe this truth?

2. Choose one verse or phrase from Acts 1—2 that stands out to you. This could be something you're intrigued by, something that makes you

uncomfortable, something that puzzles you, something that resonates with you, or just something you want to examine further. Write that here.

Going Deeper

From the Commentary

> Acts 1:8 is a key verse. To begin with, it explains that the power of the church comes from the Holy Spirit and not from man (see Zech. 4:6). God's people experienced repeated fillings of the Spirit as they faced new opportunities and obstacles (Acts 2:4; 4:8, 31; 9:17; 13:9). Ordinary people were able to do extraordinary things because the Spirit of God was at work in their lives. The ministry of the Holy Spirit is not a luxury; it is an absolute necessity.
>
> —*Be Dynamic*, page 22

3. Read the verses from Acts listed in the previous commentary excerpt. What do these verses reveal about the work of the Holy Spirit? Why is it important for us to know that the power of the church comes from the Spirit and not from man? Why is the Spirit's ministry essential to the church?

From the Commentary

What a variety of people made up that first assembly of believers! There were men and women, apostles and "ordinary" people, and even members of the Lord's earthly family (see Matt. 13:55; Mark 6:3). His "brethren" had not believed in Him during His ministry (John 7:5), but they did come to trust Him after the resurrection (Acts 1:14). Mary was there as a member of the assembly, participating in worship and prayer along with the others. The center of their fellowship was the risen Christ, and all of them adored and magnified Him.

How easy it would have been for someone to bring division into this beautiful assembly of humble people! The members of the Lord's family might have claimed special recognition, or Peter could have been criticized for his cowardly denial of the Savior. Or perhaps Peter might have blamed John because it was John who brought him into the high priest's house (John 18:15–16). John might well have reminded the others that *he* had faithfully stood at the cross, and had even been chosen by the Savior to care for His mother. But there was none of this. In fact, nobody was even arguing over who among them was the greatest!

—Be Dynamic, pages 24–25

4. What can you discern about those who were active in the early church from the first two chapters of Acts? What evidence is there that the church

was a diverse group? Why is this important? In what ways is our church today like the early church in this regard? In what ways is it different?

From Today's World

The early church was fortunate to be witness to the coming of the Holy Spirit at Pentecost. But over time, people's varying interpretations about the role of the Holy Spirit have become a matter of denominational theology. Whereas some churches barely mention the Spirit from Sunday to Sunday, others make their service all about the Holy Spirit. The differences seem to run along denominational lines, but in the time of the early church, there was no such thing as denominations—just believers desiring to become more like Christ and seeking to understand this curious gift called the Holy Spirit.

5. Why do you think denominations are so split over the role of the Holy Spirit? In what ways does this diminish the impact of Christ's church? What are the benefits of diverse interpretations of the Spirit's role and power? What can churches today learn from the coming of the Spirit at Pentecost that can help them be more effective in ministry?

From the Commentary

> The believers prayed for God's guidance before they
> "voted" because they wanted to select the man that God
> had already chosen (Prov. 16:33). Their exalted Lord was
> working in them and through them from heaven. This
> is the last instance in the Bible of the casting of lots,
> and there is no reason why believers today should use
> this approach in determining God's will. While it is not
> always easy to discover what God wants us to do, if we are
> willing to obey Him, He will reveal His will to us (John
> 7:17). What is important is that we follow the example of
> the early church by emphasizing the Word of God and
> prayer.
>
> —*Be Dynamic*, page 29

6. Why do you think the believers chose to cast lots to choose Judas's
replacement (Acts 1:26)? What's wrong with a similar approach to making
decisions today? Is there a "right" and "wrong" way to discern God's will?
Explain.

From the Commentary

As we study the events of Pentecost, it is important that we separate the accidentals from the essentials. The Spirit *came* and the people heard the sound of rushing wind and saw tongues of fire. The Spirit *baptized* and *filled* the believers, and then *spoke* as they praised God in various languages. The Spirit *empowered* Peter to preach, and then He *convicted* the listeners so that three thousand of them trusted Christ and were saved. Let's consider these ministries one by one.

—*Be Dynamic*, page 35

7. What were the "accidentals" surrounding the Pentecost? What are the essentials? Do Christians today differ on these definitions? Why? What is most significant to remember about the coming of the Holy Spirit?

From the Commentary

The baptism of the Spirit means that I belong to His body; the fullness of the Spirit means that my body belongs to

Him. The baptism is final; the fullness is repeated as we trust God for new power to witness. The baptism involves all other believers, for it makes us one in the body of Christ (Eph. 4:1–6); while the fullness is personal and individual. These are two distinct experiences and they must not be confused.

—*Be Dynamic*, page 37

8. What does it mean that the baptism of the Spirit is for all believers? What is the individual purpose of the fullness of the Spirit? How are these experiences confused? What is the result of that confusion?

From the Commentary

News travels fast in the East, and probably most of the adults in Jerusalem, residents and visitors, knew about the arrest, trial, and crucifixion of Jesus of Nazareth. They also had heard rumors of an "official announcement" that His followers had stolen the body of Jesus just to make people think that He had kept His word and been raised from the dead.

But Peter told them the truth: Jesus of Nazareth had indeed been raised from the dead, and the resurrection proves that He is the Messiah! Peter gave them four proofs of the resurrection of Jesus Christ of Nazareth, and then he called on them to believe on Christ and be saved.

—*Be Dynamic*, page 40

9. What proofs does Peter give in Acts 2 to support his claim of Jesus' resurrection? Why are these proofs important to the early church?

From the Commentary

Two phrases in Acts 2:42 may need explanation. "Breaking of bread" probably refers to their regular meals, but at the close of each meal, they probably paused to remember the Lord by observing what we call "the Lord's Supper." Bread and wine were the common fare at a Jewish table. The word *fellowship* means much more than "being together." It means "having in common" and probably refers to the sharing of material goods that was practiced in the early church. This was certainly not a form of modern communism, for the program was totally voluntary, temporary (Acts 11:27–30), and motivated by love.

The church was unified (Acts 2:44), magnified (v. 47a), and multiplied (v. 47b). It had a powerful testimony among the unsaved Jews, not only because of the miracles done by the apostles (v. 43), but also because of the way the members of the fellowship loved each other and served the Lord. The risen Lord continued to work with them (Mark 16:20), and people continued to be saved. What a church!

—*Be Dynamic*, page 43

10. Read Acts 2:42–47. What pictures do these verses paint about the role of fellowship in the early church? What were the ingredients of their fellowship? How does that compare to our churches today?

Looking Inward

Take a moment to reflect on all that you've explored thus far in this study of Acts 1—2. Review your notes and answers and think about how each of these things matters in your life today.

> *Tips for Small Groups: To get the most out of this section, form pairs or trios and have group members take turns answering these questions. Be honest and as open as you can in this discussion, but most of all, be encouraging and supportive of others. Be sensitive to those who are going through particularly difficult times and don't press for people to speak if they're uncomfortable doing so.*

11. What stands out to you about the manner in which the Holy Spirit was given to believers? What questions do you have about the Holy Spirit's role in your own life? Why is it important for you to understand the role of the Holy Spirit?

12. In what ways has your church experience been similar to and different from what you see in Acts? What aspects of the early church most appeal to you? Can you live those out today? Explain.

13. What does Jesus' resurrection mean to you? Why is His resurrection critical to faith? How is your life today affected by this truth?

Going Forward

14. Think of one or two things that you have learned that you'd like to work on in the coming week. Remember that this is all about quality, not quantity. It's better to work on one specific area of life and do it well than to work on many and do poorly (or to be so overwhelmed that you simply don't try).

Do you want to better understand the role of the Holy Spirit? Do you want to live more fully the shared life that the early church practiced? Be specific. Go back through Acts 1—2 and put a star next to the phrase or verse that is most encouraging to you. Consider memorizing this verse.

Real-Life Application Ideas: Talk with your church leaders to learn more about your church's Holy Spirit theology. If possible, have a pastor visit your small group to lead a discussion on the Holy Spirit. Bring an open mind and lots of questions and invite honest exploration of the topic. Then see if you can come up with practical applications of what you learn—ways to cooperate with the Holy Spirit in your daily life.

Seeking Help

15. Write a prayer below (or simply pray one in silence), inviting God to work on your mind and heart in those areas you've previously noted. Be honest about your desires and fears.

Notes for Small Groups:

- *Look for ways to put into practice the things you wrote in the Going Forward section. Talk with other group members about your ideas and commit to being accountable to one another.*

- *During the coming week, ask the Holy Spirit to continue to reveal truth to you from what you've read and studied.*

- *Before you start the next lesson, read Acts 3—4. For more in-depth lesson preparation, read chapters 3–4, "The Power of His Name" and "Persecution, Prayer, and Power," in* Be Dynamic.

The Name of Jesus

(ACTS 3—4)

Before you begin ...
- *Pray for the Holy Spirit to reveal truth and wisdom as you go through this lesson.*
- *Read Acts 3—4. This lesson references chapters 3–4 in* Be Dynamic. *It will be helpful for you to have your Bible and a copy of the commentary available as you work through this lesson.*

Getting Started

From the Commentary

The emphasis in Acts 3 and 4 is on the name of the Lord Jesus (Acts 3:6, 16; 4:7, 10, 12, 17–18, 30). A name, of course, implies much more than identification; it carries with it authority, reputation, and power. When somebody says, "You can use my name!" you sincerely hope the name is worth using. If an order is given in the name of the President of the United States or the Prime Minister of Great Britain, those who receive the order know that they are obligated to obey. If I were to issue orders at the White House or at No. 10 Downing Street (even if I could get in), nobody would pay much attention because my name has no official authority behind it.

But the name of the Lord Jesus has *all authority* behind it, for He is the Son of God (Matt. 28:18). Because His name is "above every name" (Phil. 2:9–11), He deserves our worship and obedience. The great concern of the first Christians was that the name of Jesus Christ, God's Son, be glorified, and believers today should have that same concern.

—Be Dynamic, page 47

1. Why would Jesus' name be so important to the early Christians? What fears might they have had about continuing His church after He ascended into heaven? How does the church continue to celebrate Jesus' name today?

More to Consider: Psalm 55:17; Daniel 6:10; and Acts 10:30 all refer to the traditional hours of prayer that Jews and those attracted to Judaism practiced. These hours were linked to the temple rites. What were the events that began to reshape the traditions that followers of Jesus were used to?

2. Choose one verse or phrase from Acts 3—4 that stands out to you. This could be something you're intrigued by, something that makes you uncomfortable, something that puzzles you, something that resonates with you, or just something you want to examine further. Write that here.

Going Deeper

From the Commentary

The contrast between Acts 2 and 3 is interesting: Peter the preacher—Peter the personal worker; multitudes— one poor man; ministry resulting in blessing—ministry resulting in arrest and persecution. The events in Acts 3 are an illustration of the last phrase in Acts 2:47, showing us how the Lord added to His church daily. While the Holy Spirit is not named in this chapter, He was certainly at work in and through the apostles, performing His ministry of glorifying Jesus Christ (John 16:14).

—*Be Dynamic*, page 48

3. What differences do you see in Peter's role between Acts 2 and 3? Why this difference? What evidence does chapter 3 give of the Holy Spirit's role, even though He's not mentioned in the chapter?

From the Commentary

In his previous sermon, Peter had explained that the cross was the meeting place of divine sovereignty and human responsibility (Acts 2:23), and he repeated this truth in this second sermon (3:17–18). There are mysteries here that the human mind cannot fully understand, so we must accept them by faith. God had a plan from all eternity, yet His plan did not force men to act against their own will. The prophets had foretold the sufferings and death of the Messiah, and the nation fulfilled these prophecies without realizing what they were doing. When God cannot rule, He overrules and always accomplishes His divine purposes and decrees.

Having announced the crime, presented the evidence, and explained the nature of their sin, Peter then offered them pardon (Acts 3:19–26)! What a strange thing for the prosecuting attorney to become the defense attorney and the pardoning judge!

—*Be Dynamic*, page 52

4. Review Acts 3:17–26. What do you think Peter's goal was in this section? What was the burden he had for the people he was speaking to? How does this message apply to us today as well?

From the Commentary

His message produced two opposite results: (1) some two thousand Jews believed the Word and were converted, and (2) the religious leaders of the nation rejected the message and tried to silence the apostles. We have here the beginning of the persecution about which Jesus had already warned His followers (Matt. 10:17–18; Luke 21:12–15; John 15:18—16:4).

—*Be Dynamic*, pages 54–55

5. Why did the religious leaders reject Peter's message? How was this the beginning of persecution? In what ways might the first result of Peter's message (the conversion of two thousand people) be related to the religious leaders' attempts to silence Peter? Does this sort of thing happen today? Explain.

From the Commentary

> The early church had none of the "advantages" that some ministries boast of and depend on today. They did not have big budgets provided by wealthy donors. Their pastors lacked credentials from the accepted schools, nor did they have the endorsement of the influential political leaders of that day. Most of their ministers had jail records and would probably have a hard time today *joining* our churches, let alone *leading* them.
>
> —*Be Dynamic*, page 61

6. What was the secret to the early church's success? (Consider the thrust of Acts 4.) How is today's church like or unlike the early church in that

regard? How might the big budgets and resources available to many of today's churches negatively affect their ability to serve as Christ's voice? How can such resources assist in the church's ministry?

From the Commentary

This was an official meeting of the Sanhedrin (Acts 4:15), the same council that a few months before had condemned Jesus to die. In fact, these officials recognized Peter and John as the associates of Jesus (Acts 4:13). The Sanhedrin was charged with the responsibility of protecting the Jewish faith, and this meant that they had to examine every new teacher and teaching that appeared in the land (see Deut. 13). They certainly had the right to investigate what the church was doing, but they did not have the right to arrest innocent men and then refuse to honestly examine the evidence.

Their question was legal, but they did everything they could to avoid admitting that a miracle had taken place (Acts 4:14). They were evasive and merely referred to the miracle as "this." They were probably scornful as well, so that their question might be paraphrased, "Where did

common people like you get the power and authority
to do a thing like this?" It was once again the question
of "By whose name?" After all, the apostles might be in
league with the Devil! Even Satan can perform miracles!

—*Be Dynamic*, page 62

7. Why would the religious leaders want to avoid referring to the miracle
that took place (4:14)? What implications did this miracle have for their
status quo? In what ways were their verbal attacks successful? In what ways
did they fail?

From the Commentary

The council was in a dilemma; no matter which way they
turned, they were "trapped." They could not deny the
miracle because the man was standing before them, and
yet they could not explain how "uneducated and untrained
men" (NASB) could perform such a mighty deed. Peter and
John were ordinary fishermen, not professional scribes or
authorized ministers of the Jewish religion. They were
disciples of Jesus of Nazareth, but—He was dead! The

council took notice of the courage and confidence of Peter and John, as well as the power of Peter's words, and it all added up to perplexity.

It is important to note that, of itself, the miracle was not proof of the resurrection of Christ or even of the truth of Peter's message. Satan can perform miracles (2 Thess. 2:9–10) and false prophets can do wonders (Deut. 13:1–5). The miracle and the message, *in the context of all that had been going on since Pentecost,* was one more evidence that Jesus Christ was alive and at work in the church by His Holy Spirit. In both sermons, Peter used the Old Testament to support and explain his claims, and this is one evidence of a true prophet of God (Deut. 13:1–5; Isa. 8:20). Miracles are not a substitute for the Word of God (Luke 16:27–31).

—Be Dynamic, page 64

8. Review 2 Thessalonians 2:9–10 and Deuteronomy 13:1–5. If false prophets and Satan can also do miracles, how did the early Christians know if a miracle was from God? How might sowing doubt about a miracle's origin have affected the early Christians? How do churches today handle apparent miracles?

More to Consider: Read Romans 13; Titus 3:1–2; 1 Peter 2:13–25. What do these passages teach us about a proper way for believers to deal with laws they don't believe in? How did the early Christians respond in a similar way to the Sanhedrin?

From the Commentary

The greatest concentration of power in Jerusalem that day was in the prayer meeting that followed the trial. This is one of the truly great prayers recorded in the Bible, and it is a good example for us to follow.

To begin with, it was a prayer that was born out of witness and service for the Lord. Peter and John had just come in "from the trenches," and the church met to pray in order to defeat the enemy. Too often today, believers gather for prayer as though attending a concert or a party. There is little sense of urgency and danger because most of us are comfortable in our Christian walk. If more of God's people were witnessing for Christ in daily life, there would be more urgency and blessing when the church meets for prayer.

—*Be Dynamic,* page 67

9. Read Acts 4:23–31. What was the main focus of this prayer? What is the urgency in the prayer? What was the result of their prayer (v. 31)?

From the Commentary

> The early church strongly believed in God's sovereignty and His perfect plan for His people. But note that they did not permit their faith in divine sovereignty to destroy human responsibility, for they were faithful to witness and pray. It is when God's people get out of balance and overemphasize either sovereignty or responsibility that the church loses power. Again, we are reminded of Augustine's wise words, "Pray as though everything depends on God, and work as though everything depended on you." Faith in a sovereign Lord is a tremendous encouragement for God's people to keep serving the Lord when the going is difficult.
>
> *—Be Dynamic,* page 69

10. As you consider Acts 4:32–37 in context, what does this tell you about the members of the early church? How does the sharing of possessions speak to their understanding of God's role in their individual lives? Their corporate lives? In what ways does today's church live out these truths?

Looking Inward

Take a moment to reflect on all that you've explored thus far in this study of Acts 3—4. Review your notes and answers and think about how each of these things matters in your life today.

> *Tips for Small Groups: To get the most out of this section, form pairs or trios and have group members take turns answering these questions. Be honest and as open as you can in this discussion, but most of all, be encouraging and supportive of others. Be sensitive to those who are going through particularly difficult times and don't press for people to speak if they're uncomfortable doing so.*

11. If Jesus is truly the "author of life" (Acts 3:15), as Peter said, what are the implications for your life? Can you imagine being transformed by this truth as Peter was? Explain.

12. In what ways is your church experience like that of the early church? Are there elements of the early church that appeal to you more than those of your current experience? List them. How can you incorporate some of the simplicity and passion of the early church into your faith experience

today? How can you strengthen these elements in your community, rather than simply regretting their lack?

13. The early church spent a lot of time in prayer. How much emphasis do you put on prayer in your personal life? In your life with other believers? What can you do to expand and improve your prayer life, both personally and corporately? How might a better prayer life affect your daily living?

Going Forward

14. Think of one or two things that you have learned that you'd like to work on in the coming week. Remember that this is all about quality, not quantity. It's better to work on one specific area of life and do it well than to work on many and do poorly (or to be so overwhelmed that you simply don't try).

Do you want to discover a richer prayer life? Do you want to be a positive influence in your faith community? Be specific. Go back through Acts 3—4 and put a star next to the phrase or verse that is most encouraging to you. Consider memorizing this verse.

Real-Life Application Ideas: Discuss with your family members or small group ways to incorporate prayer more fully into your daily schedules. Consider regular prayer times as well as ways to invite prayer in the middle of other activities such as work and even playtime. Then implement your ideas and ask God to help you grow closer to Him in the process.

Seeking Help

15. Write a prayer below (or simply pray one in silence), inviting God to work on your mind and heart in those areas you've previously noted. Be honest about your desires and fears.

Notes for Small Groups:

- *Look for ways to put into practice the things you wrote in the Going Forward section. Talk with other group members about your ideas and commit to being accountable to one another.*

- *During the coming week, ask the Holy Spirit to continue to reveal truth to you from what you've read and studied.*

- *Before you start the next lesson, read Acts 5—7. For more in-depth lesson preparation, read chapters 5–7, "Beware of the Serpent!" "Truth and Consequences," and "Stephen, the Man God Crowned," in* Be Dynamic.

The Clever Foe
(ACTS 5—7)

Before you begin ...
- *Pray for the Holy Spirit to reveal truth and wisdom as you go through this lesson.*
- *Read Acts 5—7. This lesson references chapters 5–7 in* Be Dynamic. *It will be helpful for you to have your Bible and a copy of the commentary available as you work through this lesson.*

Getting Started

From the Commentary

Satan had failed completely in his attempt to silence the witness of the church. However, the enemy never gives up; he simply changes his strategy. His first approach had been to attack the church from the outside, hoping that arrest and threats would frighten the leaders. When that failed, Satan decided to attack the church *from the inside* and use people who were a part of the fellowship.

We must face the fact that Satan is a clever foe. If he does not succeed as the devouring lion (1 Peter 5:8), then he attacks again as the deceiving serpent or an "angel of light" (2 Cor. 11:3, 13–14). Satan is both a murderer and a liar (John 8:44), and the church must be prepared for both attacks.

—*Be Dynamic,* page 75

1. Review Acts 5:1–11. What does this story teach us about how Satan attacked the early church? How is this like the way he attacks believers today?

More to Consider: Joseph, nicknamed "Barnabas," is introduced in Acts. He is mentioned at least twenty-five times in the book and another five times in the New Testament letters (Acts 9:26–27; 11:19–30; 13:1–5). Why do you think Barnabas is mentioned so often? What characteristics does he seem to have that make him a worthy subject for Luke to write about?

2. Choose one verse or phrase from Acts 5—7 that stands out to you. This could be something you're intrigued by, something that makes you uncomfortable, something that puzzles you, something that resonates with you, or just something you want to examine further. Write that here.

Going Deeper

From the Commentary

George MacDonald wrote, "Half of the misery in the world comes from trying to *look*, instead of trying to *be*, what one is not." The name that Jesus gave to this practice is "hypocrisy," which simply means "wearing a mask, playing the actor." We must not think that failure to reach our ideals is hypocrisy because no believer lives up to all that he or she knows or has in the Lord. Hypocrisy is deliberate deception, trying to make people think we are more spiritual than we really are.

When I was pastoring my first church, the Lord led us to build a new sanctuary. We were not a wealthy congregation, so our plans had to be modest. At one point in the planning, I suggested to the architect that perhaps we could build a simple edifice with a more elaborate facade at the front to make it look more like an expensive church.

"Absolutely not!" he replied. "A church stands for truth and honesty, and any church I design will not have a facade! A building should tell the truth and not pretend to be what it isn't."

—*Be Dynamic*, page 78

3. What was Ananias and Sapphira's sin in Acts 5:1–11? What sort of "front" did they put on to fool others in this story? Was God's response to this situation surprising to you? Why or why not?

From the Commentary

What is described in Acts 5 is not a case of church discipline. Rather it is an example of God's personal judgment. "The Lord shall judge his people. It is a fearful thing to fall into the hands of the living God" (Heb. 10:30–31). Had Ananias and Sapphira judged their own sin, God would not have judged them (1 Cor. 11:31), but they agreed to lie, and God had to deal with them.

Ananias was dead and buried, and Sapphira did not even know it! Satan always keeps his servants in the dark, while God guides His servants in the light (John 15:15). Peter accused her of tempting God's Spirit, that is, deliberately disobeying God and seeing how far God would go (Ex. 17:2; Deut. 6:16). They were actually defying God and daring Him to act—and He acted, with swiftness and finality. "Thou shalt not tempt the Lord thy God" (Matt. 4:7).

—*Be Dynamic*, page 81

4. Why does Luke include the story of Ananias and Sapphira in his history of the early church? What message does he seem to be giving believers? How might this picture of God's personal judgment have been received by the early Christians?

From Today's World

Nonbelievers are quick to blame the apparent hypocrisy of Christians as a reason why they don't have any interest in the church. Their finger-pointing isn't without merit, since the media is quick to pounce on stories that reveal public personalities who have vehemently taught one thing while living out the opposite. But this isn't the only reason nonbelievers have their doubts about Christianity. Many would also point to friends and neighbors who claim Christianity, but act in ways that are anything but "Christian."

5. Why does the media seem to love stories about Christians who are revealed as hypocrites? What is an appropriate response to someone who points to these stories as examples of why they don't want to have anything to do with Christianity? What are some of the challenges Christians have in general when trying to live consistent lives of faith? What's the difference between hypocrisy and simply being an imperfect human?

From the Commentary

After Pentecost, the message of the resurrection of Jesus Christ spread rapidly in Jerusalem as Spirit-empowered witnesses shared the gospel with the lost. Signs and wonders accompanied the preaching of the Word, and no one could deny that God was at work in a new way among His ancient people.

But not everybody was happy with the success of the church. The "religious establishment" that had opposed the ministry of Jesus, and then crucified Him, took the same hostile approach toward the apostles. "If they persecuted Me, they will also persecute you," said Jesus. "They will put you out of the synagogues; yes, the time is coming that whoever kills you will think that he offers God service" (John 15:20; 16:2 NKJV). These words were beginning to be fulfilled.

It was the age-old conflict between living truth and dead tradition. The new wine could not be put into the old wineskins, nor could the new cloth be sewn onto the worn-out garments (Matt. 9:14–17). The English martyr Hugh Latimer said, "Whenever you see persecution, there is more than a probability that truth is on the persecuted side."

—*Be Dynamic*, page 89

6. Review Acts 6:8—7:60. How is the story of Stephen an example of persecution in the early church? Why did the religious leaders respond so strongly to Stephen's role in the church? Does this sort of thing still happen today? Explain.

From the Commentary

> There are two words for "crown" in the New Testament: *diadema*, which means "a royal crown" and gives us the English word *diadem*; and *stephanos*, the "victor's crown," which gives us the popular name Stephen. You can inherit a *diadema*, but the only way to get a *stephanos* is to earn it.
>
> Acts 6 and 7 center on the ministry and martyrdom of Stephen, a Spirit-filled believer who was crowned by the Lord. "Be thou faithful unto death, and I will give thee a crown of life" (Rev. 2:10). He was faithful both in life and in death and therefore is a good example for us to follow.
>
> —*Be Dynamic*, page 103

7. What does it mean that Stephen was "crowned by the Lord"? What do you think the religious leaders hoped to accomplish by his death? What ended up happening? Why was Stephen's martyrdom important to the early church? To the church today?

From the Commentary

When a church faces a serious problem, this presents the leaders and the members with a number of opportunities. For one thing, problems give us the opportunity to examine our ministries and discover what changes must be made. In times of success, it is easy for us to maintain the *status quo,* but this is dangerous. Henry Ward Beecher called success "a last-year's nest from which the birds have flown." Any ministry or organization that thinks its success will go on automatically is heading for failure. We must regularly examine our lives and our ministries lest we start taking things for granted.

The apostles studied the situation and concluded that *they* were to blame: They were so busy serving tables that they were neglecting prayer and the ministry of the Word of God. They had created their own problem because they were trying to do too much. Even today, some pastors are so busy with secondary tasks that they fail to spend adequate time in study and in prayer. This creates a "spiritual deficiency" in the church that makes it easy for problems to develop.

—*Be Dynamic*, page 104

8. Back up a little and review Acts 6:1–7. What challenges did the church face during this time? What "opportunities" did these challenges present? What lessons did they learn in this process? How can the church apply these lessons today?

More to Consider: Read Luke 23:34, 46; and Acts 7:59–60. How are
the words Stephen spoke as he was being stoned similar to Jesus' prayer
as He was being crucified? Is this coincidence or purposeful? What
does this teach us about forgiveness?

From the Commentary

Jews from many nations resided in Jerusalem in their own
"quarters," and some of these ethnic groups had their own
synagogues. The freedmen ("libertines") were the descen-
dants of Jews who had previously been in bondage but
had won their freedom from Rome. Since Paul came from
Tarsus in Cilicia (Acts 21:39), it is possible that he heard
Stephen in the synagogue and may have debated with
him. However, nobody could match or resist Stephen's
wisdom and power (see Luke 21:15). Their only alterna-
tive was to destroy him.

Their treatment of Stephen parallels the way the Jewish
leaders treated Jesus. First, they hired false witnesses to
testify against him. Then, they stirred up the people who
accused him of attacking the law of Moses and the temple.
Finally, after listening to his witness, they executed him
(see Matt. 26:59–62; John 2:19–22).

—*Be Dynamic*, page 106

9. Review Acts 6:8–15. What does it mean that the religious leaders
couldn't "stand up against [Stephen's] wisdom or the Spirit by whom he

spoke"? What was their argument with Stephen? What was their response to Stephen's ministry? What made them so threatened by it?

From the Commentary

> Acts 7:1–53 is the longest address in the book of Acts and one of the most important. In it, Stephen reviewed the history of Israel and the contributions made by their revered leaders: Abraham (Acts 7:2–8), Joseph (vv. 9–17), Moses (vv. 18–44), Joshua (v. 45), and David and Solomon (vv. 46–50).

> But this address was more than a recitation of familiar facts; it was also a refutation of their indictments against Stephen and a revelation of their own national sins. Stephen proved from their own Scriptures that the Jewish nation was guilty of worse sins than those they had accused him of committing.

> —*Be Dynamic*, page 107

10. Review Acts 7. What stands out to you about Stephen's discourse in this chapter? What approach did Stephen take to respond to the allegations

against him? What lessons can we learn from this address to help us when we're wrongly accused?

Looking Inward

Take a moment to reflect on all that you've explored thus far in this study of Acts 5—7. Review your notes and answers and think about how each of these things matters in your life today.

> *Tips for Small Groups: To get the most out of this section, form pairs or trios and have group members take turns answering these questions. Be honest and as open as you can in this discussion, but most of all, be encouraging and supportive of others. Be sensitive to those who are going through particularly difficult times and don't press for people to speak if they're uncomfortable doing so.*

11. What was your emotional response to the story of Ananias and Sapphira? When have you felt the temptation to do something for "show" rather than out of sincerity? If you gave into that temptation, what was the result? What lesson does the story of Ananias and Sapphira have for you?

12. What are some of the hypocrisies you've witnessed in the church or in the lives of its members? Have you ever confronted someone's hypocrisy? If so, how did you do this? What was the result? What is a believer's responsibility when he or she discovers hypocrisy in a fellow believer?

13. Put yourself in Stephen's shoes. What might your response have been had you been accused as he was? Is it easy for you to stand up for what you believe when being attacked? Why or why not? What gave Stephen the strength to speak the truth? What can you learn from his life that can help you live out your faith boldly?

Going Forward

14. Think of one or two things that you have learned that you'd like to work on in the coming week. Remember that this is all about quality, not quantity. It's better to work on one specific area of life and do it well than

to work on many and do poorly (or to be so overwhelmed that you simply don't try).

Do you want to understand what it means to live boldly like Stephen? Be specific. Go back through Acts 5—7 and put a star next to the phrase or verse that is most encouraging to you. Consider memorizing this verse.

Real-Life Application Ideas: Spend a week trying to notice ways you put up a front to impress or otherwise deceive others. Ask the Holy Spirit to help you notice. When you notice yourself doing this, don't beat up on yourself. (That's a substitute for real repentance.) Instead, ask God for forgiveness and the grace to change. And accept His forgiveness with gratitude.

Seeking Help

15. Write a prayer below (or simply pray one in silence), inviting God to work on your mind and heart in those areas you've previously noted. Be honest about your desires and fears.

Notes for Small Groups:

- *Look for ways to put into practice the things you wrote in the Going Forward section. Talk with other group members about your ideas and commit to being accountable to one another.*

- *During the coming week, ask the Holy Spirit to continue to reveal truth to you from what you've read and studied.*

- *Before you start the next lesson, read Acts 8—12. For more in-depth lesson preparation, read chapters 8–12, "A Church on the Move," "God Arrests Saul," "Peter's Miracle Ministry," "Making Room for the Gentiles," and "Wake Up to a Miracle!" in* Be Dynamic.

Becoming Salt
(ACTS 8—12)

Before you begin ...
- *Pray for the Holy Spirit to reveal truth and wisdom as you go through this lesson.*
- *Read Acts 8—12. This lesson references chapters 8–12 in* Be Dynamic. *It will be helpful for you to have your Bible and a copy of the commentary available as you work through this lesson.*

Getting Started

From the Commentary

"There is one thing stronger than all the armies in the world," wrote Victor Hugo, "and that is an idea whose time has come."

The gospel of Jesus Christ is much more than an idea. The gospel is "the power of God to salvation for everyone who believes" (Rom. 1:16 NKJV). It is God's "dynamite" for breaking down sin's barriers and setting the prisoners free. Its time had come and the church was on the move. The "salt" was now leaving the "Jerusalem saltshaker" to be spread over all Judea and Samaria, just as the Lord had commanded (Acts 1:8).

The events in Acts 8 center around four different men: Saul (8:1–3); Philip (8:4–8); Simon the Sorcerer (8:9–25); and an Ethiopian (8:26–40).

—*Be Dynamic,* page 117

1. Review each of the men featured in Acts 8 (Saul, Philip, Simon the Sorcerer, the Ethiopian). What were their stories? What stands out to you about each man and the role he played in the early church story? What lessons do these stories teach us about the challenges and opportunities of being a Christ-follower?

More to Consider: Read Acts 9:1–2. What prompted Saul's continued zeal? Why was he so angry with the Christ-followers?

2. Choose one verse or phrase from Acts 8—12 that stands out to you. This could be something you're intrigued by, something that makes you uncomfortable, something that puzzles you, something that resonates with you, or just something you want to examine further. Write that here.

Going Deeper

From the Commentary

The Lord had a special work for Saul to do (Acts 26:16–18). The Hebrew of the Hebrews would become the apostle to the Gentiles; the persecutor would become a preacher; and the legalistic Pharisee would become the great proclaimer of the grace of God. Up to now, Saul had been like a wild animal, fighting against the goads, but now he would become a vessel of honor, the Lord's "tool," to preach the gospel in the regions beyond. What a transformation!

Some thirty years later, Paul wrote that Christ had "apprehended him" on the Damascus road (Phil. 3:12). Saul was

out to arrest others when the Lord arrested him. He had
to lose his religion before he could gain the righteousness
of Christ.

—*Be Dynamic*, page 133

3. Why do you think God chose Saul, the persecutor, to become one of
His greatest proclaimers? What does this say about how God sees us?
About how God chooses to go about bringing His plan to fruition? What
are some examples today of men and women who made similar drastic
changes in their lives?

From the Commentary

Acts 9:15 is a good summary of Paul's life and ministry.
It was all of grace, for he did not choose God; it was God
who chose him (2 Thess. 2:13). He was God's vessel (2
Tim. 2:20–21), and God would work in and through him
to accomplish His purposes (Eph. 2:10; Phil. 2:12–13).
God's name would be glorified as His servant would take
the gospel to Jews and Gentiles, kings and commoners,
and as he would suffer for Christ's sake. This is the first

reference in the book of Acts to the gospel going to the Gentiles (see also Acts 22:21; 26:17).

—Be Dynamic, page 135

4. Why is it important in the context of the early church's history that God chose Saul and not the other way around? How does this play into the shift from a Jewish-only sect to a group of believers that includes Gentiles?

From the Commentary

> Saul immediately began to proclaim the Christ that he had persecuted, declaring boldly that Jesus is the Son of God. This is the only place in Acts that you find this title, but Paul used it in his epistles at least fifteen times. It was a major emphasis in his ministry. The dramatic change in Saul's life was a source of wonder to the Jews at Damascus. Every new convert's witness for Christ ought to begin right where he is, so Saul began his ministry first in Damascus (Acts 26:20).
>
> *—Be Dynamic*, page 137

5. How might the Jews in Damascus have initially responded to Saul's sudden conversion and bold claim about Jesus? In what ways are people today similarly suspect when a critic of Christianity suddenly starts to proclaim the truth? What does Paul's proclamation teach us about the power of God? About the manner in which believers ought to respond to the life-changing power of God?

From the Commentary

We usually think of the apostles as leaders who told other people what to do, but often the people commanded them! (For Peter's "philosophy of ministry" read 1 Peter 5.) Peter was a leader who served the people and was ready to respond to their call. Peter had the power to heal, and he used the power to glorify God and help people, not to promote himself.

It was a Jewish custom first to wash the dead body, and then to anoint it with spices for burial. When Peter arrived in the upper room where Dorcas lay in state, he found a group of weeping widows who had been helped by her ministry. Keep in mind that there was no "government aid" in those days for either widows or orphans, and needy people had to depend on their "network" for assistance. The church has an obligation to help people who are truly in need (1 Tim. 5:3–16; James 1:27).

The account of Peter's raising of Dorcas should be compared with the account of our Lord's raising of Jairus's daughter (Mark 5:34–43). In both cases, the mourning people were put out of the room, and the words spoken are almost identical: "*talitha cumi:* little girl, arise"; "*Tabitha cumi:* Tabitha, arise." Jesus took the girl by the hand before He spoke to her, for He was not afraid of becoming ceremonially defiled, and Peter took Dorcas by the hand after she had come to life. In both instances, it was the power of God that raised the person from the dead, for the dead person certainly could not exercise faith.

As with the healing of Aeneas, the raising of Dorcas attracted great attention and resulted in many people trusting Jesus Christ.

—Be Dynamic, pages 147–48

6. Review Acts 9:32–43 and read Mark 5:35–43. How is the account of Peter's raising of Dorcas like Jesus' raising of Jairus's daughter? Is this significant? Why or why not? How did the crowds respond in each of these stories? What lessons did these events teach God's people?

From the Commentary

> Acts 11 describes how the church in Jerusalem related to
> "the saints below," the Gentiles in Caesarea and Antioch
> who had trusted Jesus Christ as their Savior and Lord.
> Having fellowship with the Gentiles was a new experi-
> ence for these Jewish Christians, who all their lives had
> looked on the Gentiles as pagans and outsiders. Tradition
> said that a Gentile had to "become a Jew" in order to be
> accepted, but now Jews and Gentiles were united in the
> church through faith in Jesus Christ (Gal. 3:26–28).
>
> —*Be Dynamic*, page 159

7. Review Acts 11. Why did the Jewish Christians look down on the
Gentiles? In what ways are there similar divisions among Christians today?
How did Peter answer the concerns of the Jewish Christians? How ought
we respond today to Christians who look down on other believers because
they don't follow similar practices or do certain things?

From the Commentary

> Acts 11:24 gives us a "spiritual profile" of Barnabas, and he appears to be the kind of Christian all of us would do well to emulate. He was a righteous man who obeyed the Word in daily life so that his character was above reproach. He was filled with the Spirit, which explains the effectiveness of his ministry. That he was a man of faith is evident from the way he encouraged the church and then encouraged Saul. New Christians and new churches need people like Barnabas to encourage them in their growth and ministry.
>
> *—Be Dynamic,* page 163

8. How did Barnabas encourage the new Gentile believers (Acts 11:19–30)? What approach did he take when worshipping with them? What can we learn from his example for how we should treat new believers and new church members?

More to Consider: It was at Antioch that the name "Christian" was first applied to the disciples of Jesus Christ. The Latin suffix -ian means "belonging to the party of." In derision, some of the pagan citizens of Antioch joined this Latin suffix to the Hebrew name "Christ" and came up with Christian. The name is found only three times in the New Testament: Acts 11:26; 26:28; 1 Peter 4:16. If the name "Christian" was coined in derision, why did it become the common reference for those who are followers of Christ?

From the Commentary

The pattern for Christian giving today is not Acts 2:44–45 and 4:31–35 but Acts 11:29, "every man according to his ability." It is this pattern that Paul taught in 2 Corinthians 8—9. The practice of "Christian communism" was found only in Jerusalem and was a temporary measure while the message was going "to the Jew first." Like God's care of the Jews in the wilderness, it was a living exhibition of the blessings God would bestow if the nation would repent and believe.

—Be Dynamic, page 167

9. Read Acts 2:44–45 and 4:31–35, as well as Acts 11:29–30. Why is the example of giving "according to ability" a better picture of Christian giving? How do we determine what we are able to give, as distinct from giving God what's left over after we have paid for what we want? Does this model in Acts 11 line up with what you know about how your own church is funded? If not, why do you think this is true?

From the Commentary

If you were chained to two Roman soldiers and facing the possibility of being executed the next day, would you sleep very soundly? Probably not, but Peter did. In fact, Peter was so sound asleep that the angel had to strike him on the side to wake him up! ...

Peter had been a prisoner twice before ... but this prison experience was different from the other two. This time, he was alone, and the deliverance did not come right away. The other two times, he was able to witness, but this time, no special witnessing opportunities appeared. Peter's previous arrests had taken place after great victories, but this one followed the death of James, his dear friend and colleague. It was a new situation altogether.

—*Be Dynamic*, pages 175–76

10. Read Acts 12:1–19. What gave Peter such confidence and peace in the midst of this trial? What are the sorts of trials Christians face today that might be similar to what Peter endured? How can we learn to respond with confidence and peace to those trials?

Looking Inward

Take a moment to reflect on all that you've explored thus far in this study of Acts 8—12. Review your notes and answers and think about how each of these things matters in your life today.

Tips for Small Groups: To get the most out of this section, form pairs or trios and have group members take turns answering these questions. Be honest and as open as you can in this discussion, but most of all, be encouraging and supportive of others. Be sensitive to those who are going through particularly difficult times and don't press for people to speak if they're uncomfortable doing so.

11. As you read through Acts 8, which of the four men represented in that chapter do you most relate to? Why? What can you learn from each of these stories to help you live out your faith daily?

12. Think back on the time before you knew Christ. What are some of the character traits you had then that God now uses to further His kingdom through you? What are some of the characteristics you've changed since your conversion? In what ways are you most like Paul? Least like Paul?

13. The Jewish Christians tended to look down on Gentile Christians. Are there groups of Christians that you look down on? Why? How can you change that attitude so that you honor their faith, even if you disagree with some of their practices?

Going Forward

14. Think of one or two things that you have learned that you'd like to work on in the coming week. Remember that this is all about quality, not quantity. It's better to work on one specific area of life and do it well than to work on many and do poorly (or to be so overwhelmed that you simply don't try).

Do you want to learn how to be as bold as Paul? Be specific. Go back through Acts 8—12 and put a star next to the phrase or verse that is most encouraging to you. Consider memorizing this verse.

Real-Life Application Ideas: Paul's conversion was radical and set the table for significant growth in the early Christian church. Think back to the time when you first believed. How does your enthusiasm and "fire" for the faith compare today? If you feel like it's fizzled a bit, consider ways to stoke the flames and rediscover your passion and boldness. Talk with church leaders. Brainstorm things you can do not only to grow your intellectual understanding of the faith, but also ideas for growing your experience of practical faith (serving others, reaching out in evangelism, etc.).

Seeking Help

15. Write a prayer below (or simply pray one in silence), inviting God to work on your mind and heart in those areas you've previously noted. Be honest about your desires and fears.

Notes for Small Groups:

- *Look for ways to put into practice the things you wrote in the Going Forward section. Talk with other group members about your ideas and commit to being accountable to one another.*
- *During the coming week, ask the Holy Spirit to continue to reveal truth to you from what you've read and studied.*
- *Before you start the next lesson, read Acts 13—16. For more in-depth lesson preparation, read chapters 1–3, "God Opens the Doors," "Don't Close the Doors!" and "More Open Doors," in* Be Daring.

Paul Begins His Ministry
(ACTS 13—16)

Before you begin …
- *Pray for the Holy Spirit to reveal truth and wisdom as you go through this lesson.*
- *Read Acts 13—16. This lesson references chapters 1–3 in* Be Daring. *It will be helpful for you to have your Bible and a copy of the commentary available as you work through this lesson.*

Getting Started

From the Commentary

We usually identify the preaching of the gospel with the quiet rural villages of Palestine where the Lord Jesus ministered. For this reason, many Christians are surprised to learn that the church in the book of Acts was almost entirely *urban*. Historian Wayne A. Meeks writes that "within a decade of the crucifixion of Jesus, the village culture of Palestine had been left behind, and the Greco-Roman city became the dominant environment of the Christian movement" (*The First Urban Christians*, 11).

The church began in Jerusalem and then spread to other cities including Samaria, Damascus, Caesarea, and Antioch in Syria. At least forty different cities are named in Acts. From Antioch, Paul and his helpers carried the gospel throughout the then-known world. In fact, the record given in Acts 13—28 is almost a review of ancient geography. About the year 56, the apostle Paul was able to write, "So that from Jerusalem, and round about unto Illyricum, I have fully preached the gospel of Christ" (Rom. 15:19). What a record!

—*Be Daring*, page 13

1. In Acts 13—14, Luke describes Paul's ministry in six different cities. What stands out to you about the different ministry needs and approaches in these cities? How were these cities and their circumstances like cities today? How were they different?

More to Consider: Acts 13:1–3 shows that the believers in Antioch viewed evangelism as such a priority that they sent out some of their top leaders to do that work. Why is it often hard for individuals and churches to invest heavily in outreach as opposed to taking care of their own? How can you treat outreach as a priority?

2. Choose one verse or phrase from Acts 13—16 that stands out to you. This could be something you're intrigued by, something that makes you uncomfortable, something that puzzles you, something that resonates with you, or just something you want to examine further. Write that here.

Going Deeper

From the Commentary

On their return trip to Antioch, the missionaries were engaged in several important ministries.

First, they preached the gospel and made disciples ("taught many"). It is difficult to understand how they got back into the cities from which they had been expelled, but the Lord opened the doors.

Second, they strengthened ("confirmed") the believers in the things of Christ and encouraged ("exhorted") them to continue in the faith. Continuance is a proof of true faith in Jesus Christ (John 8:31–32; Acts 2:42). Paul made it very clear that living the Christian life was not an easy thing and that they would all have to expect trials and sufferings before they would see the Lord in glory.

Third, they organized the churches (Acts 14:23–25). The local church is both an organism and an organization, for if an organism is not organized, it will die! Paul and Barnabas ordained spiritual leaders and gave them the responsibility of caring for the flock. If you compare Titus 1:5 and 7, you will see that "elder" and "bishop" (overseer) refer to the same office, and both are equivalent to "pastor" (shepherd).

The word translated *ordained* means "to elect by a show of hands." It is possible that Paul chose the men and the congregation voted its approval, or that the people selected them by vote and Paul ordained them (see Acts 6:1–6).

Finally, they reported to their "sending church" on the work God had done (Acts 14:26–28). They had been gone at least a year, and it must have been exciting for them and for the church when they arrived back home. They had, by the grace of God, fulfilled the work God had given them to do, and they joyfully reported the blessings to the church family.

—Be Daring, page 22

3. Read Acts 14:21–28. Why was each of these activities of Paul's mission team important to the growth of the early church? Do churches work in a similar way today? Why or why not? What can today's church learn from Paul's missionary trip and subsequent ministry in Antioch?

From the Commentary

It all started when some legalistic Jewish teachers came to Antioch and taught that the Gentiles, in order to be saved, had to be circumcised and obey the law of Moses. These men were associated with the Jerusalem congregation but not authorized by it (Acts 15:24). Identified with the Pharisees (Acts 15:5), these teachers were "false brethren" who wanted to rob both Jewish and Gentile believers of their liberty in Christ (Gal. 2:1–10; 5:1ff.).

It is not surprising that there were people in the Jerusalem church who were strong advocates of the law of Moses but ignorant of the relationship between law and grace. These people were Jews who had been trained to respect and obey the law of Moses, and after all, Romans, Galatians, and Hebrews had not yet been written! There was a large group of priests in the Jerusalem assembly (Acts 6:7), as well as people who still followed some of the Old Testament practices (see Acts 21:20–26). It was a time of transition, and such times are always difficult.

—*Be Daring*, pages 27–28

4. Read Acts 15:1–5. What prompted these Jewish teachers to tell the Gentiles they needed to be circumcised in order to be saved? What did they have to gain by teaching this? Are there similar scenarios in today's church? Describe them. What would Paul say to the people in today's church who teach about additional requirements for salvation?

From the Commentary

Paul and Barnabas reported on the present (Acts 15:12). Peter's witness made a great impact on the congregation because they sat in silence after he was finished. Then Paul and Barnabas stood up and told the group what God had done among the Gentiles through their witness. Dr. Luke devoted only one summary sentence to their report since he had already given it in detail in Acts 13—14. Paul and Barnabas were greatly respected by the church (see Acts 15:25–26), and their testimony carried a great deal of weight.

Their emphasis was on the miracles that God had enabled them to perform among the Gentiles. These miracles were proof that God was working with them (Mark 16:20; Acts 15:4) and that they were God's chosen messengers (Rom. 15:18–19; Heb. 2:2–4). "Does God give you his Spirit and work miracles among you because you observe the law, or because you believe what you heard?" (Gal. 3:5 NIV). They had preached grace, not law, and God had honored this message.

—Be Daring, page 31

5. Read Acts 15:1–21. What does this section of Acts tell us about how the church wrestled with the challenges they faced? How did the testimony of Paul, Barnabas, and Peter influence the discussion regarding the Gentiles? What role did Scripture play (Acts 15:15–18)?

From the Commentary

The leaders and the whole church (Acts 15:22), directed by the Holy Spirit (Acts 15:28), made a twofold decision: a doctrinal decision about salvation, and a practical decision about how to live the Christian life.

The doctrinal decision we have already examined. The church concluded that Jews and Gentiles are all sinners before God and can be saved only by faith in Jesus Christ. There is one need, and there is but one gospel to meet that need (Gal. 1:6–12). God has today but one program: He is calling out a people for His name. Israel is set aside but not cast away (Rom. 11:1ff.), and when God's program for the church is completed, He will begin to fulfill His kingdom promises to the Jews.

But all doctrine must lead to duty. James emphasized this in his epistle (James 2:14–26), and so did Paul in his letters. It is not enough for us simply to accept a biblical truth; we must apply it personally in everyday life. Church problems are not solved by passing resolutions, but by practicing the revelations God gives us from His Word.

—Be Daring, page 34

6. Acts 15:22–35 describes the details of the letter the church sent to the Gentile believers. What specific concerns does this letter speak to? Why these concerns? In what ways does it emphasize the practical aspects of a

life of faith? What sort of letter might the leaders of your church write to its members today?

From the Commentary

We today can learn a great deal from this difficult experience of the early church. To begin with, problems and differences are opportunities for growth just as much as temptations for dissension and division. Churches need to work together and take time to listen, love, and learn. How many hurtful fights and splits could have been avoided if only some of God's people had given the Spirit time to speak and to work.

Most divisions are caused by "followers" and "leaders." A powerful leader gets a following, refuses to give in on even the smallest matter, and before long there is a split. Most church problems are not caused by doctrinal differences but by different viewpoints on practical matters. What color shall we paint the church kitchen? Can we change the order of the service? I heard of one church that almost split over whether the organ or the piano should be on the right side of the platform! Christians need to learn the art of loving compromise.

—*Be Daring*, pages 36–37

7. Review Acts 15:9–35. What can today's church learn from how the early church dealt with this conflict? What role did prayer play in their examination of the difficult experience? What are some of the problems churches face today that require careful, prayerful consideration? Why is it often the little things that divide churches?

From the Commentary

For the apostle Paul, the church at Antioch was not a parking lot; it was a launching pad. He could never settle down to a "comfortable ministry" anywhere as long as there were open doors for the preaching of the gospel.

Paul would have agreed enthusiastically with the words of Robertson McQuilken from his book *The Great Omission:* "In a world in which nine out of every ten people are lost, three out of four have never heard the way out, and one of every two cannot hear, the church sleeps on. Could it be we think there must be some other way? Or perhaps we don't really care that much." Paul cared—and so should we.

—Be Daring, page 41

8. What was behind the split between Paul and Barnabas in Acts 15:36–41? Why do you think Paul left without Barnabas? What does this situation tell us about each of these men?

More to Consider: What benefit did Paul gain by partnering up with Silas for his subsequent missionary journeys? Note: Silas was a chief man in the church, a prophet (Acts 15:22, 32), one chosen to take the Jerusalem Conference decrees to the churches (Acts 15:27) and, like Paul, a Roman citizen (Acts 16:37).

From the Commentary

Paul and Silas approached their destination from the east, so they came first to Derbe and then to Lystra, just the reverse of the first journey (Acts 14:6–20). The preachers went from church to church, delivering the decrees and helping establish the believers in the faith. The result was fruit from the witness of the believers so that the churches increased in number daily (see Acts 2:47). It was certainly a most successful tour, but I wonder if any of the believers asked about Barnabas. And what did Paul tell them?

Perhaps the best thing that happened at Lystra was the enlistment of Timothy to replace John Mark as Paul's special assistant. Timothy was probably converted through Paul's ministry when the apostle first visited Lystra, for Paul called him "my beloved son" (1 Cor. 4:17) and "my own son in the faith" (1 Tim. 1:2). Timothy's mother and grandmother had prepared the way for his decision by being the first in the family to trust Christ (2 Tim. 1:5). Young Timothy undoubtedly witnessed Paul's sufferings in Lystra (Acts 14:19–20; 2 Tim. 3:10–11) and was drawn by the Lord to the apostle. Timothy was Paul's favorite companion and coworker (Phil. 2:19–23), perhaps the son Paul never had but always wanted.

—*Be Daring*, page 43

9. Why was it valuable for Paul to enlist Timothy as his assistant? What value would his youth have provided the missionaries? What does this decision tell us about the importance of listening to young people in the church today?

From the Commentary

As you review Acts 16, you can see that the work of the Lord progresses through difficulties and challenges. Sometimes the workers have problems with each other, and sometimes the problems come from the outside. It is also worth noting that not every sinner comes to Christ in exactly the same manner. Timothy was saved partly through the influence of a godly mother and grandmother. Lydia was converted through a quiet conversation with Paul at a Jewish prayer meeting, while the jailer's conversion was dramatic. One minute he was a potential suicide, and the next minute he was a child of God!

—*Be Daring*, page 50

10. Review Acts 16. What do we learn about Paul through his experience with the jailer? What can we learn about God's grace in this chapter? What can we learn about how God uses His people to change lives?

Looking Inward

Take a moment to reflect on all that you've explored thus far in this study of Acts 13—16. Review your notes and answers and think about how each of these things matters in your life today.

Tips for Small Groups: To get the most out of this section, form pairs or trios and have group members take turns answering these questions. Be honest and as open as you can in this discussion, but most of all, be encouraging and supportive of others. Be sensitive to those who are going through particularly difficult times and don't press for people to speak if they're uncomfortable doing so.

11. As you consider Paul's first missionary trip, what stands out to you about his fervor for the Lord? When have you felt a similar fervor? Have you ever been called to any kind of missions work? If so, how did you respond to that call?

12. What sort of expectations do you have of other Christians' behavior or lifestyle choices? What causes you to have expectations like this? Is it wrong to expect certain behaviors of other Christians? Why or why not?

How are your expectations like and unlike the false leaders' rules requiring Christians to become Jewish before they could be saved?

13. Who are the "Pauls" in your life? (The mentors who have helped you grow in your faith.) Who are the "Timothys"? (Those you've mentored.) Why is important to have a spiritual mentor? What is the value of mentoring others?

Going Forward

14. Think of one or two things that you have learned that you'd like to work on in the coming week. Remember that this is all about quality, not quantity. It's better to work on one specific area of life and do it well than to work on many and do poorly (or to be so overwhelmed that you simply don't try).

Do you want to find someone who can mentor you? Do you want to be more intentional with your evangelism, perhaps with a partner or a team? Be specific. Go back through Acts 13—16 and put a star next to the phrase or verse that is most encouraging to you. Consider memorizing this verse.

Real-Life Application Ideas: If you don't already have a spiritual mentor, seek one out. Look for someone who's been a Christian longer than you have—someone you look up to and trust. If he or she agrees to be your mentor, work together to come up with a plan for spending time together so you can learn about what it means to mature in the faith.

Seeking Help

15. Write a prayer below (or simply pray one in silence), inviting God to work on your mind and heart in those areas you've previously noted. Be honest about your desires and fears.

Notes for Small Groups:

- *Look for ways to put into practice the things you wrote in the Going Forward section. Talk with other group members about your ideas and commit to being accountable to one another.*

- *During the coming week, ask the Holy Spirit to continue to reveal truth to you from what you've read and studied.*

- *Before you start the next lesson, read Acts 17—18. For more in-depth lesson preparation, read chapters 4–5, "Responding to God's Word" and "It's Always Too Soon to Quit," in* Be Daring.

Another Journey
(ACTS 17—18)

Before you begin ...
- *Pray for the Holy Spirit to reveal truth and wisdom as you go through this lesson.*
- *Read Acts 17—18. This lesson references chapters 4–5 in* Be Daring. *It will be helpful for you to have your Bible and a copy of the commentary available as you work through this lesson.*

Getting Started

From the Commentary

Following the famous Egnatian Way, Paul and Silas went one hundred miles from Philippi to Thessalonica. (Timothy is not mentioned again until Acts 17:14, so he may have remained in Philippi.) As far as we can tell, they did not pause to minister in either Amphipolis or Apollonia. Perhaps there were no synagogues in those cities, and Paul certainly expected the new believers in Philippi to carry the message to their neighbors. It was

Paul's policy to minister in the larger cities and make them centers for evangelizing a whole district (see Acts 19:10, 26; 1 Thess. 1:8).

Paul knew that Thessalonica (our modern Salonika) was a strategic city for the work of the Lord. Not only was it the capital of Macedonia, but it was also a center for business, rivaled only by Corinth. It was located on several important trade routes, and it boasted an excellent harbor. The city was predominantly Greek, even though it was controlled by Rome. Thessalonica was a "free city," which meant that it had an elected citizens' assembly, it could mint its own coins, and it had no Roman garrison within its walls....

As the result of three weeks' ministry, Paul saw a large number of people believe, especially Greek proselytes and influential women. Among the men were Aristarchus and Secundus, who later traveled with Paul (Acts 20:4). Luke's phrase "not a few" (Acts 17:4, 12) is one way of saying, "It was a big crowd!"

—Be Daring, pages 53–55

1. Why do you think Paul's missionary trips were so effective? What can you glean from Acts 17 about Paul's approach to missions? What lessons can we learn from Paul's approach that can be applied to our churches today?

More to Consider: The Greek word translated another *in 17:7 means "another of a different kind," that is, a king unlike Caesar. Why would the news about a "different" king cause such a ruckus among the Jews?*

2. Choose one verse or phrase from Acts 17—18 that stands out to you. This could be something you're intrigued by, something that makes you uncomfortable, something that puzzles you, something that resonates with you, or just something you want to examine further. Write that here.

Going Deeper

From the Commentary

Under cover of night, Paul and Silas left Thessalonica and headed for Berea, about forty-five miles away. It does not appear that Timothy was with them, as he was probably working in Philippi. Later, he would join Paul in Athens (Acts 17:15) and then be sent to Thessalonica to encourage the church in its time of persecution (1 Thess. 3:1ff.). Since Timothy was a Gentile, and had not been present when the trouble erupted, he could minister in the city freely. The peace bond could keep Paul out, but it would not apply to Paul's young assistant.

Paul went into the synagogue and there discovered a group of people keenly interested in the study of the Old Testament Scriptures. In fact, they met *daily* to search the Scriptures to determine whether or not what Paul was saying was true. Paul had been overjoyed at the way the people in Thessalonica had received the Word (1 Thess. 2:13), so these "noble Bereans" must have really encouraged his heart. All of us should imitate these Bereans by faithfully studying God's Word daily, discussing it, and testing the messages that we hear.

God used His Word so that many people trusted Christ.

—*Be Daring*, page 56

3. Why did Luke refer to the Bereans as being of "noble character"? What would this "noble character" look like in today's believers? Why did the troublemakers in Thessalonica follow Paul to Berea? What was the result of the troublemakers' efforts? How is this like the way some people cause trouble in churches today?

From the Commentary

Paul arrived in the great city of Athens, not as a sightseer, but as a soul winner. The late Noel O. Lyons, for many years director of the Greater Europe Mission, used to say, "Europe is looked over by millions of visitors and is overlooked by millions of Christians." Europe needs the gospel today just as it did in Paul's day, and we dare not miss our opportunities. Like Paul, we must have open eyes and broken hearts.

Athens was in a period of decline at this time, though still recognized as a center of culture and education. The glory of its politics and commerce had long since faded. It had a famous university and numerous beautiful buildings, but it was not the influential city it once had been. The city was given over to a "cultured paganism" that was nourished by idolatry, novelty, and philosophy (Acts 17:16, 21).

—*Be Daring*, page 57

4. Read 17:16–34. What was Paul's initial impression of Athens? What approach did he take in ministering to the people there? What can we learn from Paul's approach that can help us reach out to nonbelievers today?

From Today's World

Christianity may be the world's largest religion, but it's also the media's most popular target when it comes to criticism and ridicule. Whether it's the national news delivering a story about a pastor's fall from grace or a television show or movie poking fun at the practices of faith, Christianity is often portrayed as a religion of hypocrites and fools. Certainly there are those in the church who make themselves easy targets for ridicule, but they don't represent the majority of believers.

5. Why is Christianity so often the target of ridicule? What is a right response to these sorts of portrayals of the faith? How does the media's typical portrayal of Christianity affect the way in which you relate to non-Christians?

From the Commentary

When you contrast the seeming meager results in Athens with the great harvests in Thessalonica and Berea, you are tempted to conclude that Paul's ministry there was a dismal failure. If you do, you might find yourself drawing a hasty and erroneous conclusion. Paul was not told to leave, so we assume he lingered in Athens and continued to minister to both believers and unbelievers. Proud, sophisticated, wise Athenians would not take easily to Paul's humbling message of the gospel, especially when he summarized all of Greek history in the phrase "the times of this ignorance." The soil here was not deep and it contained many weeds, but there was a small harvest.

And after all, one soul is worth the whole world!

—*Be Daring*, page 63

6. Read Acts 17:16–34 and compare the experience in Athens to that in Thessalonica (17:1–9) and Berea (17:10–15). Why was the experience in Athens so dramatically different for Paul? What was unique about the audiences Paul spoke to in the different towns?

From the Commentary

Paul came to Corinth following his ministry to the philosophers in Greece, and he determined to magnify Jesus Christ and the cross, to depend on the Holy Spirit, and to present the gospel in simplicity (1 Cor. 2:1–5). There were many philosophers and itinerant teachers in

Corinth, preying on the ignorant and superstitious population, and Paul's message and ministry could easily be misunderstood.

One way Paul separated himself from the "religious hucksters" was by supporting himself as a tentmaker. By the providence of God, he met a Jewish couple, Aquila and Priscilla ("Prisca," 2 Tim. 4:19), who were workers in leather as was Paul. Jewish rabbis did not accept money from their students but earned their way by practicing a trade. All Jewish boys were expected to learn a trade, no matter what profession they might enter. "He who does not teach his son to work, teaches him to steal!" said the rabbis, so Saul of Tarsus learned to make leather tents and to support himself in his ministry (see Acts 18:3; 1 Cor. 9:6–15; 2 Cor. 11:6–10).

—Be Daring, page 68

7. How might Paul's experience in Athens have affected his approach to the people in Corinth? Why is it notable that Acts tells about Paul's trade as a tentmaker? How might this trade have helped Paul in his missionary journey?

From the Commentary

Whenever God is blessing a ministry, you can expect increased opposition as well as increased opportunities. "For a great and effective door has opened to me, and there are many adversaries" (1 Cor. 16:9 NKJV). After all, the enemy gets angry when we invade his territory and liberate his slaves. As in Thessalonica and Berea (Acts 17:5–13), the unbelieving Jews who rejected the Word stirred up trouble for Paul and his friends (see 1 Thess. 2:14–16). Such opposition is usually proof that God is at work, and this ought to encourage us. Spurgeon used to say that "the Devil never kicks a dead horse!"

Jewish opposition had forced Paul to leave Thessalonica and Berea, but in Corinth, it only made him determined to stay there and get the job done. It is always too soon to quit! Like the undaunted Christopher Columbus, Paul could write in his journal, "Today we sailed on!"

—*Be Daring*, pages 69–70

8. Read Acts 18:9–11. What does this passage tell us about Paul's experience in Corinth? After the dream, Paul stayed for a year and a half. What does this tell us about Paul's faith? About God's promise and protection of Paul?

More to Consider: To have blood on your hands means that you bear the responsibility for another's death. The image comes from the watchman on the city walls whose task it was to stay alert and warn of coming danger (Ezek. 3:17–21; 33:1–9). Review Acts 18:6. What does it mean to have "blood on your head" (see also Josh. 2:19)?

From the Commentary

The conversion of Crispus, an important Jewish leader, opened up more opportunities for evangelism and brought more opposition from the enemy! The Jewish community in Corinth was no doubt furious at Paul's success and did everything possible to silence him and get rid of him. Dr. Luke does not give us the details, but I get the impression that between Acts 18:8 and 9, the situation became especially difficult and dangerous. Paul may have been thinking about leaving the city when the Lord came to him and gave him the assurance that he needed.

It is just like our Lord to speak to us when we need Him the most. His tender "Fear not!" can calm the storm in our hearts regardless of the circumstances around us. This is the way He assured Abraham (Gen. 15:1), Isaac (Gen. 26:24), and Jacob (Gen. 46:3), as well as Jehoshaphat (2 Chron. 20:15–17) and Daniel (Dan. 10:12, 19), Mary (Luke 1:30), and Peter (Luke 5:10). The next time you feel alone and defeated, meditate on Hebrews 13:5 and

Isaiah 41:10 and 43:1–7, and claim by faith the presence
of the Lord. He is with you!

—*Be Daring*, page 72

9. Read the passages in the previous commentary excerpt. How does each
of these offer us assurance? How might some of these same passages have
helped to assure Paul in his journey?

From the Commentary

Cenchraea was the seaport for Corinth, and there was
a Christian congregation there (Rom. 16:1). Here Paul
had his head shorn, "for he had a vow." This probably
refers to the Nazarite vow described in Numbers 6.
Since the Nazarite vow was purely voluntary, Paul was
not abandoning grace for law when he undertook it.
The vow was not a matter of salvation but of personal
devotion to the Lord. He allowed his hair to grow for a
specific length of time and then cut it when the vow was
completed. He also abstained from using the fruit of the
vine in any form.

We are not told why Paul took this vow. Perhaps it was a part of his special dedication to God during the difficult days of the early ministry in Corinth. Or perhaps the vow was an expression of gratitude to God for all that He had done for him and his associates. According to Jewish law, the Nazarite vow had to be completed in Jerusalem with the offering of the proper sacrifices. The hair was shorn at the completion of the vow, not at the beginning, and it was not necessary for one to be in Jerusalem to make the vow.

Luke does not tell us how long Paul was in Ephesus, but the time was evidently very short. The Jews there were much more receptive to the gospel and wanted Paul to stay, but he wanted to get to Jerusalem to complete his vow, and then to Antioch to report to the church. However, he did promise to return, and he kept that promise (Acts 19:1).

—*Be Daring*, page 76

10. When Paul had his head shaved, it could have appeared to some that he was doing this in order to comply with the law. What does Paul's action teach us about the importance of following through on commitments? How might this have confused people about the "requirements" of salvation?

Looking Inward

Take a moment to reflect on all that you've explored thus far in this study of Acts 17—18. Review your notes and answers and think about how each of these things matters in your life today.

Tips for Small Groups: To get the most out of this section, form pairs or trios and have group members take turns answering these questions. Be honest and as open as you can in this discussion, but most of all, be encouraging and supportive of others. Be sensitive to those who are going through particularly difficult times and don't press for people to speak if they're uncomfortable doing so.

11. What excites you most about evangelism? What scares you? How might your missionary journey be different from Paul's? What approach can you take toward sharing the good news? What help do you need from a partner or a team?

12. Paul's experience in Athens was less effective than his previous stops. When have you felt like Paul did in Athens? How do you deal with the frustrations that come when people just don't understand what you're

saying? What are some creative ways to share the message of Christ that people in any culture or circumstance can understand?

13. Have you ever been the object of ridicule because of your faith? How did you respond to that ridicule? What are some practical ways to deal with people who make fun of your beliefs?

Going Forward

14. Think of one or two things that you have learned that you'd like to work on in the coming week. Remember that this is all about quality, not quantity. It's better to work on one specific area of life and do it well than to work on many and do poorly (or to be so overwhelmed that you simply don't try).

Do you want to learn how to respond to ridicule? Be specific. Go back through Acts 17—18 and put a star next to the phrase or verse that is most encouraging to you. Consider memorizing this verse.

Real-Life Application Ideas: Spend time studying Paul's ministry to Athens (Acts 17:16–34), then think of ways you can better reach out to people who have philosophical disagreements with your beliefs. Is it best to confront these people directly? If so, consider how well you're prepared. Study the Scriptures. Talk with trusted leaders. Learn how to respond wisely to those who would tend to make fun of your faith. Then spend lots of time in prayer and ask God for wisdom so you can respond appropriately when confronted. Also, consider how you can reach out to such people in relationship if their philosophical disagreement is more of a smoke screen than genuine inquiry.

Seeking Help

15. Write a prayer below (or simply pray one in silence), inviting God to work on your mind and heart in those areas you've previously noted. Be honest about your desires and fears.

Notes for Small Groups:

- *Look for ways to put into practice the things you wrote in the Going Forward section. Talk with other group members about your ideas and commit to being accountable to one another.*

- *During the coming week, ask the Holy Spirit to continue to reveal truth to you from what you've read and studied.*

- *Before you start the next lesson, read Acts 19—22. For more in-depth lesson preparation, read chapters 6–8, "Excitement in Ephesus," "A Minister's Farewell," and "The Misunderstood Missionary," in* Be Daring.

Ephesus and After

(ACTS 19—22)

Before you begin ...
- *Pray for the Holy Spirit to reveal truth and wisdom as you go through this lesson.*
- *Read Acts 19—22. This lesson references chapters 6–8 in* Be Daring. *It will be helpful for you to have your Bible and a copy of the commentary available as you work through this lesson.*

Getting Started

From the Commentary

When Paul departed from Ephesus for Jerusalem, he left his friends Aquila and Priscilla behind to carry on the witness in the synagogue. Imagine their surprise one Sabbath to hear a visiting Jewish teacher named Apollos preach many of the truths that they themselves believed and taught!

Apollos was certainly an exceptional man in many ways. He came from Alexandria, the second most important city in the Roman Empire. A center for education and philosophy, the city was founded by (and named after) Alexander the Great, and it boasted a university with a library of almost 700,000 volumes. The population of Alexandria (about 600,000) was quite cosmopolitan, being made up of Egyptians, Romans, Greeks, and Jews. At least a quarter of the population was Jewish, and the Jewish community was very influential.

Apollos knew the Old Testament Scriptures well and was able to teach them with eloquence and power. He was fervent ("boiling") in his spirit and diligent in his presentation of the message. He was bold enough to enter the synagogue and preach to the Jews. The only problem was that this enthusiastic man was declaring an incomplete gospel.

—Be Daring, page 82

1. Why was Apollos' gospel incomplete? What was he missing in his message (Acts 19:1–7)? What is the danger of preaching an incomplete gospel?

More to Consider: The Ephesian temple was probably four centuries old in Paul's day. In the sacred enclosure of the temple stood the "sacred image" of Artemis (a wilderness and fertility goddess) that was supposed to have fallen from heaven (Acts 19:35). How might the pagan setting in this city have affected Paul's preaching? What unique challenges might he have faced in a city with such a significant pagan presence?

2. Choose one verse or phrase from Acts 19—22 that stands out to you. This could be something you're intrigued by, something that makes you uncomfortable, something that puzzles you, something that resonates with you, or just something you want to examine further. Write that here.

Going Deeper

From the Commentary

When Paul arrived back in Ephesus, he met twelve men who professed to be Christian "disciples" but whose lives gave evidence that something was lacking. Paul asked them, "Did you receive the Holy Spirit when you believed?" (Acts 19:2 NIV, NASB, NKJV). The question was important because *the witness of the Spirit is the one indispensable proof that a person is truly born again* (Rom. 8:9, 16; 1 John 5:9–13), and you receive the Spirit when you believe on Jesus Christ (Eph. 1:13).

Their reply revealed the vagueness and uncertainty of their faith, for they did not even know that the Holy Spirit had been given! As disciples of John the Baptist, they knew that there was a Holy Spirit, and that the Spirit would one day baptize God's people (Matt. 3:11; Luke 3:16; John 1:32–33). It is possible that these men were Apollos' early "converts" and therefore did not fully understand what Christ had done.

—*Be Daring*, page 84

3. Read Acts 19:1–10. What does this passage tell us about the role of the Holy Spirit? About our responsibility in sharing not only the "good news" but also how the Holy Spirit works? How well does your church do in teaching about the Holy Spirit? What are some ways your church could do a better job in teaching the complete gospel?

From the Commentary

It is remarkable that Paul was able to witness in the synagogue for three months before he had to leave. No doubt the faithful ministry of Aquila and Priscilla played an important part in this success. However, hardness of heart set in (Heb. 3:7ff.), so Paul left the synagogue and moved his ministry to a schoolroom, taking his disciples with him. He probably used the room during the "off hours" each day (11:00 a.m. to 4:00 p.m.), when many people would be resting. Paul ministered in this way for about two years and "all they [who] dwelt in Asia heard the word of the Lord Jesus, both Jews and Greeks" (Acts 19:10).

What a victorious ministry! It appears that everybody knew what Paul was saying and doing (see Acts 19:17, 20)! Even Paul's enemies had to admit that the Word was spreading and people were being saved (Acts 19:26). Two factors made this possible: the witness of the believers as they went from place to place, and the "special miracles" that God enabled Paul to perform in Ephesus (Acts 19:11).

—*Be Daring*, page 87

4. Read Acts 19:11–20. Why couldn't the Jews successfully exorcise the evil spirits? Why did this frighten the Jews? What does this section of Scripture teach us about the way in which God's power is manifest?

From the Commentary

In the final third of the book of Acts, Dr. Luke records Paul's journey to Jerusalem, his arrest there, and his voyage to Rome. The gospel of Luke follows a similar pattern as Luke describes Christ's journey to Jerusalem to die (Luke 9:53; 13:33; 18:31; 19:11, 28). Much as Jesus set His face "like a flint" to do the Father's will (Isa. 50:7; Luke 9:51), so Paul determined to finish his course with joy, no matter what the cost might be (Acts 20:24).

"I do not expect to visit this country again!" D. L. Moody spoke those words in 1867 when he made his first trip to England. He was so seasick during the voyage that he decided he would never sail again, but he made five more visits to England, seasickness notwithstanding.

Paul was ready for another journey. He wanted to make at least one more visit to the churches the Lord had helped him to found, because Paul was a man with a concerned heart. "The care of all the churches" was his greatest joy as well as his heaviest burden (2 Cor. 11:23–28).

—*Be Daring*, page 95

5. Review Acts 20. How do these events compare to the previous aspects of Paul's missionary experience? What are the key messages in his farewell to the Ephesian elders (Acts 20:17–38)? What role does prayer play in this farewell?

From the Commentary

Paul was not able to make it to Jerusalem for the annual Passover celebration, so now his goal was to arrive there at least by Pentecost (Acts 20:16). Note the pronoun change to "us" and "we," for Dr. Luke has now joined the party (see Acts 16:17). He had probably been ministering at Philippi where he joined Paul for the last leg of the journey. Paul must have rejoiced to have Luke, Titus, and Timothy at his side again. The men remained at Troas a week so that they might fellowship with the believers there. Perhaps they were also waiting for the departure of the next ship.

Luke gives us a brief report of a local church service in Troas, and from it we learn something of how they met and worshipped the Lord.

—*Be Daring,* pages 96–97

6. Review Acts 20:6–12. What were the elements of the church service in Troas? How does this compare to a modern church service?

From the Commentary

> The word *elder* is *presbutos* in the Greek ("presbyter")
> and refers to a mature person who has been selected to
> serve in office (Acts 14:23). These same people are called
> "overseers" in Acts 20:28, which is *episkopos* or "bishop."
> They were chosen to "feed the church" (Acts 20:28),
> which means "to shepherd." Paul called the local church
> "a flock" (Acts 20:28–29), so these men were also pastors.
> (The word *pastor* means "shepherd.") Thus in the New
> Testament churches, the three titles *elder, bishop,* and *pastor* were synonymous.
>
> —*Be Daring*, page 100

7. Read 1 Timothy 3:1–7 and Titus 1:5–9. What do these passages say
about the qualifications for someone to be an elder? Why would Paul
choose to speak specifically to the elders when preparing to leave Ephesus?
Who are the elders in your church? How is their role like and unlike that
which is described here?

More to Consider: Read Acts 20:28–38. Paul brought his farewell message to a close by warning the leaders of the dangers they had to recognize and deal with if they were to protect and lead the church. What dangers was he referring to? What are the dangers today's church needs to warn against?

From the Commentary

Paul had devoted a good part of his third missionary journey to taking up a love gift for the Jews in Judea. It was a practical way for the Gentiles to show their oneness with their Jewish brothers and sisters, and to repay them for sharing the gospel with the Gentiles (Rom. 15:25–27). There was in the church a constant threat of division, for the Jewish extremists (the Judaizers) wanted the Gentiles to live like Jews and follow the law of Moses (Acts 15:1ff.). Wherever Paul ministered, these extremists tried to hinder his work and steal his converts. Paul hoped that his visit to Jerusalem with the offering would help to strengthen the fellowship between Jews and Gentiles.

—Be Daring, page 110

8. Why didn't Paul and his missionary team follow the counsel of the disciples in Tyre and Caesarea (Acts 21:4, 12)? If, as Luke states, the disciples in Tyre were led by the Spirit to counsel Paul, what does Paul's reluctance to heed their advice say about him? What does this say about how God was working in both the disciples and Paul?

From the Commentary

You get the impression that the legalists in the Jerusalem church had been working behind the scenes. No sooner had Paul finished his report than the elders brought up the rumors that were then being circulated about Paul among the Jewish Christians. It has well been said that, though a rumor doesn't have a leg to stand on, it travels mighty fast!

What were his enemies saying about Paul? Almost the same things they had said about Jesus and Stephen: He was teaching the Jews to forsake the laws and customs given by Moses and the fathers. They were not worried about what Paul taught the Gentile believers, because the relationship of the Gentiles to the law had been settled at the Jerusalem Conference (Acts 15). In fact, the elders carefully rehearsed the matter (Acts 21:25), probably for the sake of Paul's Gentile companions. The leaders were especially concerned that Paul's presence in the city not cause division or disruption among the "thousands of Jews ... zealous of the law" (Acts 21:20).

—Be Daring, pages 113–14

9. Why were so many believing Jews still clinging to the law of Moses? What was attractive about the law of Moses in comparison with the message Paul was preaching?

From the Commentary

Paul's entire time in Jerusalem was one filled with serious misunderstandings, but he pressed on. Perhaps at this point some of his friends were saying, "We told him so! We warned him!" For Paul and his associates, it may have looked like the end of the road, but God had other plans for them. Paul would witness again and again, and to people he could never have met had he not been a Roman prisoner. God's missionary did get to Rome—and the Romans paid the bill!

That's what happens when God's people are willing to be daring!

—Be Daring, page 120

10. What were some of the ways the Jews misunderstood Paul's ministry (Acts 21:27—22:29)? Why were the Jews in Jerusalem threatened by Paul? How is Paul's experience in Jerusalem similar to the way Jesus was treated?

Looking Inward

Take a moment to reflect on all that you've explored thus far in this study of Acts 19—22. Review your notes and answers and think about how each of these things matters in your life today.

Tips for Small Groups: To get the most out of this section, form pairs or trios and have group members take turns answering these questions. Be honest and as open as you can in this discussion, but most of all, be encouraging and supportive of others. Be sensitive to those who are going through particularly difficult times and don't press for people to speak if they're uncomfortable doing so.

11. How well acquainted are you with the work of the Holy Spirit? If you were talking with a non-Christian, would you be able to confidently express the Spirit's role? Which aspects of the faith are most difficult for you to explain?

12. Describe a time when you confidently shared your faith with someone else. What was that experience like? Where did you find your confidence? What was the result of that interaction? Now think about a time when

you were less confident about your faith. How did that conversation play out?

13. In what areas of life, if any, do you tend toward legalism? Why do you think you're tempted toward these things? How might Paul counsel you in these areas?

Going Forward

14. Think of one or two things that you have learned that you'd like to work on in the coming week. Remember that this is all about quality, not quantity. It's better to work on one specific area of life and do it well than to work on many and do poorly (or to be so overwhelmed that you simply don't try).

Do you need to avoid being legalistic in any areas of your faith? Be specific. Go back through Acts 19—22 and put a star next to the phrase or verse that is most encouraging to you. Consider memorizing this verse.

Real-Life Application Ideas: If you don't already know what the qualifications are to become an elder in your church, ask a church leader to share them. Then take a look at the qualifications and see how your faith life "measures up." Whether or not you could ever be an elder, are there ways you can mature in your faith so you could be considered "elder-like"? Work on those areas of your faith life.

Seeking Help

15. Write a prayer below (or simply pray one in silence), inviting God to work on your mind and heart in those areas you've previously noted. Be honest about your desires and fears.

Notes for Small Groups:

- *Look for ways to put into practice the things you wrote in the Going Forward section. Talk with other group members about your ideas and commit to being accountable to one another.*

- *During the coming week, ask the Holy Spirit to continue to reveal truth to you from what you've read and studied.*

- *Before you start the next lesson, read Acts 23—28. For more in-depth lesson preparation, read chapters 9–12, "Paul the Prisoner," "Paul the Witness," "Paul the Defender," and "Paul Arrives in Rome," in* Be Daring.

The Prisoner
(ACTS 23—28)

Before you begin ...
- *Pray for the Holy Spirit to reveal truth and wisdom as you go through this lesson.*
- *Read Acts 23—28. This lesson references chapters 9–12 in* Be Daring. *It will be helpful for you to have your Bible and a copy of the commentary available as you work through this lesson.*

Getting Started

From the Commentary

"Paul the prisoner" (Acts 23:18) was the name the Roman soldiers used for the apostle, a designation he himself often used (Eph. 3:1; 4:1; 2 Tim. 1:8; Philem. 1, 9). Paul was under "military custody," which meant he was bound to a Roman soldier who was responsible for him. Prisoners under "public custody" were put in the common jail, a horrible place for any human being to suffer (Acts 16:19–24).

—*Be Daring,* page 123

1. As you read about Paul's trial and imprisonment, what sense do you get about Paul's demeanor? What gave him the ability to be calm in the face of the charges and then after he was imprisoned? After all Paul had gone through, it wouldn't be surprising if he felt frustrated or like giving up. Instead, he pressed on. What lesson can we learn from his endurance that's applicable to today's church?

More to Consider: Paul's friends could visit him and help meet his personal needs, but there is no record that the Jerusalem church took any steps to assist him, either in Jerusalem or during his two years in Caesarea. Do you think this is because no one visited him, or merely because it wasn't recorded? What are the implications in either case?

2. Choose one verse or phrase from Acts 23—28 that stands out to you. This could be something you're intrigued by, something that makes you uncomfortable, something that puzzles you, something that resonates with you, or just something you want to examine further. Write that here.

Going Deeper

From the Commentary

Having discovered that Paul was a Roman citizen, the Roman captain now had two serious problems to solve. First, he needed to let the prisoner know what the official charges were against him, since that was Paul's right as a Roman citizen. Second, he also needed to have some official charges for his own records and to share with his superiors. He was sure that Paul had done something notorious, otherwise why would so many people want to do away with him? Yet nobody seemed to know what Paul's crimes were. What a plight for a Roman official to be in!

The logical thing was to let Paul's own people try him, so the captain arranged for a special meeting of the Jewish council (Sanhedrin). This group was composed of seventy (or seventy-one) of the leading Jewish teachers, with the high priest presiding. It was their responsibility to interpret and apply the sacred Jewish law to the affairs of the nation, and to try those who violated that law. The Romans gave the council permission to impose capital punishment where the offense deserved it.

—Be Daring, page 124

3. Read Acts 23:1–2. What is your reaction to the way the Sanhedrin acted toward Paul? What was Paul's reaction (v. 3)? Paul didn't realize at first

that he was speaking to the high priest. How might his response have been different if he had?

From the Commentary

Having failed in his personal approach, Paul then used a doctrinal approach. He declared that the real issue was his faith in the doctrine of the resurrection, a doctrine over which the Pharisees and Sadducees violently disagreed. Paul knew that by defending this important doctrine, he would divide the council and soon have the members disputing among themselves, which is exactly what happened. So violent was the response that Claudius and his men had to rush down to the floor of the council chamber and rescue their prisoner for the second time!

—*Be Daring*, page 127

4. Review Acts 23:6–10. Why did Paul shift to the doctrinal approach in his defense? Do you think he expected a fair trial? If not, what would he have to gain by addressing the doctrine of the resurrection? What was his motive for this?

From the Commentary

"Law was the most characteristic and lasting expression of the Roman spirit," wrote historian Will Durant in *Caesar and Christ*. "The first person in Roman law was the citizen." In other words, it was the responsibility of the court to protect the citizen from the State, but too often various kinds of corruption infected the system and made justice difficult for the common man. Paul would soon discover how corrupt a Roman governor could be.

"The Roman secret of government was the principle of indirect rule," wrote Arnold Toynbee. This meant that the real burden of administration was pretty much left on the shoulders of the local authorities. Imperial Rome got involved only if there was danger from without or if the local governing units were at odds with one another.

In Acts 24 we see the Roman legal system at work.

—*Be Daring*, page 135

5. What can you learn about the Roman legal system from Acts 24? How does it compare with your country's current legal system? How did the legal system play into Paul's circumstance in Jerusalem? In what ways is this like and unlike the way the Roman legal system played out in Jesus' story?

More to Consider: Compare Luke's account of Paul's arrest (Acts 21:27–40) with the captain's account (Acts 23:25–30) and the lawyer's account (Acts 24:5–8). What does each of these accounts tell you? What does this reveal about the challenges of the legal system? About the challenges of uncovering the truth of Paul's story?

From the Commentary

Paul closed his defense by replying to the members of the Jewish council (Acts 24:20–21). Instead of giving him a fair hearing, the high priest and the Sanhedrin had abused him and refused to hear him out. Ananias was no doubt grateful that Paul said nothing about his slap in the face, for it was not legal for a Roman citizen to be treated that way.

Do we detect a bit of holy sarcasm in Paul's closing statement? We might paraphrase it, "If I have done anything evil, it is probably this: I reminded the Jewish council of our great Jewish doctrine of the resurrection." Remember, the book of Acts is a record of the early church's witness to the resurrection of Jesus Christ (Acts 1:22). The Sadducees had long abandoned the doctrine, and the Pharisees did not give it the practical importance it deserved. Of course, Paul would have related this doctrine to the resurrection of Jesus Christ, and the Sanhedrin did not want that.

—*Be Daring*, page 142

6. What do we learn about Paul in his response to Felix (Acts 24:10–21)? How does he use this situation to further the cause of Christ? Again, Paul references the resurrection as a key point in his argument. What does this tell us about our own approach to sharing the good news?

From the Commentary

The new governor, Porcius Festus, was a better man than his predecessor and took up his duties with the intention of doing what was right. However, he soon discovered that Jewish politics was not easy to handle, especially the two-year-old case of the apostle Paul, a prisoner with no official charges against him. Paul was a Jew whose countrymen wanted to kill him, and he was a Roman whose government did not know what to do with him.

—*Be Daring*, page 149

7. What was Festus's dilemma concerning Paul (Acts 25—26)? How did Festus ultimately respond to the case of Paul's imprisonment (see especially 26:24)? What was King Agrippa's role in determining Paul's fate? What ultimately kept Paul from being sentenced to death?

From the Commentary

"I must also see Rome!" Those were Paul's words during
his ministry in Ephesus (Acts 19:21), and little did he realize all that would happen to him before he would arrive in
the imperial city: illegal arrest, Roman and Jewish trials,
confinement, and even shipwreck. He had long wanted
to preach the gospel in Rome (Rom. 1:14–16) and then
go on into Spain (Rom. 15:28), but he had not planned
to travel as a prisoner. Through it all, Paul trusted God's
promise that he would witness in Rome (Acts 23:11), and
the Lord saw him through.

Why would Luke devote such a long section of his book
to a description of a voyage and shipwreck? Surely he
could have summarized the account for us! But Luke
was a skilled writer, inspired by the Spirit of God, and
he knew what he was doing. For one thing, this exciting
report balances the speeches that we have been reading
and brings more drama into the account. Also, Luke was
an accurate historian who presented the important facts
about his hero and his voyage to Rome.

—*Be Daring*, page 163

8. Why would Luke devote such a long section of Acts to a description of
a voyage and a shipwreck (Acts 27—28)? How does this section of Acts
add drama to the account of Paul's ministry? Why might that be of value
to the reader?

From the Commentary

> Paul was not the only prisoner that Julius and his men were taking to Rome, for there were "certain other prisoners" with them. The Greek word means "others of a different kind" and may suggest that, unlike Paul, these men were going to Rome to die and not to stand trial. What mercy that they met Paul who could tell them how to go to heaven when they died!
>
> The centurion found a coastal ship leaving Caesarea, so they embarked and covered the eighty miles from Caesarea to Sidon in one day. In Sidon, Paul was permitted to visit his friends and put together the things needed for the long trip. Luke records the kindness of a Roman officer to the apostle Paul (Acts 24:23), as well as the encouragement of the anonymous believers in Sidon. Their names are in God's book and they shall be rewarded one day (Phil. 4:3).
>
> *—Be Daring*, pages 164–65

9. Review Acts 27:1–20. How does this description of Paul's voyage help us understand Paul's role in God's plan? What does it tell us about the culture of the day? Why is that relevant to Christians today?

From the Commentary

> God had brought them to the Isle of Malta (which means "refuge"), where the native people welcomed all 276 of them and did their best to make them comfortable. To the Greeks, anybody who did not speak Greek was a "barbarian." These people proved to be kind and sympathetic. The storm abated, but the weather was cold, so the natives built a fire.
>
> After all he had done for the passengers, Paul could well have requested a throne and insisted that everybody serve him! Instead, he did his share of the work and helped gather fuel for the fire. No task is too small for the servant of God who has the mind of Christ (Phil. 2:1–13).
>
> —*Be Daring*, page 169

10. Why might the islanders on Malta have chosen to show "unusual kindness" to Paul (Acts 28:2)? Why does Luke include the story of the viper (28:3–6)? What can we learn about dealing with trials by the way Paul handled his imprisonment (28:17–20)?

Looking Inward

Take a moment to reflect on all that you've explored thus far in this study of Acts 23—28. Review your notes and answers and think about how each of these things matters in your life today.

Tips for Small Groups: To get the most out of this section, form pairs or trios and have group members take turns answering these questions. Be honest and as open as you can in this discussion, but most of all, be encouraging and supportive of others. Be sensitive to those who are going through particularly difficult times and don't press for people to speak if they're uncomfortable doing so.

11. Have you ever been in a situation similar to Paul when he was on trial for his faith and ministry? If so, how did you deal with it? What role did your faith play when you were listening to or responding to accusers?

12. How comfortable would you be offering a "doctrinal defense" of your faith? What elements of doctrine are you comfortable discussing? Which are most difficult for you? What are practical things you can do to get to know doctrine better so you have a ready defense should you ever find yourself challenged?

13. As you look back on Paul's long, often difficult life, what stands out to you about the manner in which he presented himself? In what ways are you on a missionary journey? What are the trials you're facing? How will you press on in spite of them?

Going Forward

14. Think of one or two things that you have learned that you'd like to work on in the coming week. Remember that this is all about quality, not quantity. It's better to work on one specific area of life and do it well than to work on many and do poorly (or to be so overwhelmed that you simply don't try).

Do you want to learn how to be more like Paul in his response to hardship and opposition? Be specific. Go back through Acts 23—28 and put a star next to the phrase or verse that is most encouraging to you. Consider memorizing this verse.

Real-Life Application Ideas: Plan a "missionary journey" of your own. Begin in prayer, asking God to lead you as you consider what your journey might look like. Then discuss the idea with friends who might also join you. This doesn't have to be a journey across a great distance—it might just be a walk in your neighborhood. As you come up with a plan, share the details with group members so they can support you in prayer. Then go boldly out into the world and be a minister for Christ!

Seeking Help

15. Write a prayer below (or simply pray one in silence), inviting God to work on your mind and heart in those areas you've previously noted. Be honest about your desires and fears.

Notes for Small Groups:

- *Look for ways to put into practice the things you wrote in the Going Forward section. Talk with other group members about your ideas and commit to being accountable to one another.*
- *During the coming week, ask the Holy Spirit to continue to reveal truth to you from what you've read and studied.*

Summary and Review

Notes for Small Groups: This session is a summary and review of this book. Because of that, it is shorter than the previous lessons. If you are using this in a small-group setting, consider combining this lesson with a time of fellowship or a shared meal.

> *Before you begin…*
> - *Pray for the Holy Spirit to reveal truth and wisdom as you go through this lesson.*
> - *Briefly review the notes you made in the previous sessions. You will refer back to previous sections throughout this bonus lesson.*

Looking Back

1. Over the past eight lessons, you've explored the book of Acts. What expectations did you bring to this study? In what ways were those expectations met?

2. What is the most significant personal discovery you've made from this study?

3. What surprised you most about the early church? What, if anything, troubled you?

Progress Report

4. Take a few moments to review the Going Forward sections of the previous lessons. How would you rate your progress for each of the things you chose to work on? What adjustments, if any, do you need to make to continue on the path toward spiritual maturity?

5. In what ways have you grown closer to Christ during this study? Take a moment to celebrate those things. Then think of areas where you feel you still need to grow and note those here. Make plans to revisit this study in a few weeks to review your growing faith.

Things to Pray About

6. Acts is a history book as well as a teaching book. As you reflect on both the rich history and the wealth of teaching, ask God to reveal to you those truths that you most need to hear. Revisit the book often and seek the Holy Spirit's guidance to gain a better understanding of what it means to be a member of God's true church.

7. Acts introduces the early church and Paul's role in helping to grow the church. As you read about Paul's life, what stands out to you about his

commitment to the church? What lessons can we learn from Paul that can inspire church leaders today?

8. Whether you've been studying this in a small group or on your own, there are many other Christians working through the very same issues you discovered when examining the book of Acts. Take time to pray for each of them, that God would reveal truth, that the Holy Spirit would guide you, and that each person might grow in spiritual maturity according to God's will.

A Blessing of Encouragement

Studying the Bible is one of the best ways to learn how to be more like Christ. Thanks for taking this step. In closing, let this blessing precede you and follow you into the next week while you continue to marinate in God's Word:

May God light your path to greater understanding as you review the truths found in the book of Acts and consider how they can help you grow closer to Christ.

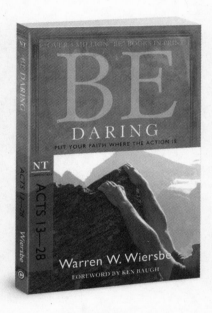